W9-BZD-883

An Irrepressible Hope

NOTES FROM CHICAGO CATHOLICS

Edited by Claire Bushey

Artwork by Franklin McMahon

acta
PUBLICATIONS
Chicago, Illinois

AN IRREPRESSIBLE HOPE
Notes from Chicago Catholics
Edited by Claire Bushey

Artwork by Franklin McMahon, courtesy of Mary Irene McMahon
and Margot McMahon

Cover and text design by Patricia A. Lynch

Questions for reflection and discussion for personal and group use
on the articles in this book are available online at no charge at
www.actapublications.com.

Note: Because this book contains so many references to the Catholic church,
both "big C" and little "c," the word *church* is lowercased even when it refers
to the church as an institution. While *church* is often capitalized in religious
contexts, the accepted practice in publishing, according to *The Chicago Manual
of Style*, is to make the first letter lowercase, and we have followed that practice
throughout this book.

Copyright © 2012 by Claire Bushey

Published by ACTA Publications, 4848 N. Clark Street, Chicago, IL 60640,
(800) 397-2282, www.actapublications.com

Library of Congress Number: 2012952045
ISBN: 978-0-87946-500-1
Printed in the United States of America by Versa Press
Year 25 24 23 22 21 20 19 18 17 16 15 14 13 12
Printing 20 19 18 17 16 15 14 13 12 11 10 9 8 7 6 5 4 3 2 First

A portion of the royalties for this book will be donated to the National Center
for the Laity.

CONTENTS

REDEMPTION

An irrepressible hope

Some books want to be written. They force their way from conception to execution to publication through a series of serendipitous events. This book is one of them.

The idea for this collection of essays started with a small clutch of priests sitting around talking with Greg Pierce, the publisher at ACTA Publications. Cardinal Francis George had submitted his pro forma resignation a few months earlier, and the priests, a loose group of friends and colleagues steeped in the ethos of Vatican II and stationed at parishes throughout the Chicago area, were feeling pessimistic about the direction of the church in general and who might succeed Cardinal George in particular. Worse than pessimistic, they felt powerless.

Let's write a book, Pierce suggested, and tell the world (and the next archbishop) what Catholicism in Chicago is all about.

The project took shape within days. The book would be a series of snapshots, brief but telling anecdotes from Chicago Catholics that would illustrate for our new archbishop, whoever he might be, and for anyone else who might be wondering, the nature of our church and city, so that he might come to know his flock. Taken collectively, these essays from pew-sitters and pulpit-pounders alike would document the splendid variety and vibrancy of the Chicago Catholic church at this moment in its history. Perhaps someone would send a copy of the book to the Papal Nuncio in Washington that might educate and edify him as he considered possible candidates to fill the see. Once his decision was made and ratified in Rome, a copy could find its way to the new archbishop too. For this unnamed, distant prelate, who would in some approaching year arrive at the skyscrapered shores of Lake Michigan, we would bare our peculiar souls.

E-mails were sent, enthusiasm kindled. And over the next week it slowly dawned on Pierce exactly how much work he'd added to his to-do list. At that uncomfortable moment, with reality setting in, I showed up.

I wasn't a book editor. I was and am a journalist by trade, a group not traditionally known as the most God-fearing of people. (Once I interviewed a minister who, when I alluded to Jesus's advice to the rich young man, gave me a pleased but puzzled smile before explaining that most reporters he talked to weren't terribly familiar with the Bible.) Yet I am a prodigal only recently returned to Holy Mother Church following years of trying to be anything else than Catholic. Chicago is a place where these aspects of my personality, Catholic and journalist, mesh well; it's a town that allows for questions and that places justice at the center of faith. But heading into the summer of 2012, I was looking to branch out into the book publishing industry and so e-mailed a number of Chicago publishers looking for part-time work. Most didn't respond. Pierce wrote back in twenty-seven minutes. A day later, I'd taken over the essay acquisition and editing of the book. It's a cliché to say God works in mysterious ways, but that doesn't mean it isn't true.

Since then, I've raised one or two eyebrows from friends and colleagues after explaining the project to them. Basically, their amusement boils down to this: The Vatican does not care what we have to say. By describing our own experiences of faith and how they might affect what we want from an archbishop, we're proffering input unsolicited. It's the old the-Catholic-church-is-not-a-democracy argument. Why bother with an answer if nobody asked a question?

It's true that some experiences contained within this book—and the conclusions the writers draw from them—will be more familiar and acceptable to the current church hierarchy than others. I tried to solicit a range of subject matter for this collection, from essays that celebrate our common ground as Catholics, like the centrality of the

Eucharist to our faith, to stories about women's ordination and homosexuality that illuminate the terrain of our differences.

As I read these essays I see great pride in Chicago, in our shared communion across parishes and with the larger Catholic universe, as well as an irrepressible hope for what we might carry forward into the future until the day it can be claimed. Because while I do not expect the powers-that-be to select Chicago's next archbishop based on the wisdom in this slim volume, I do believe this: An idea is a durable thing. It lays around, strewn on the floor of the cultural consciousness until the day it is needed, when an individual or a society or even a religion picks it up, dusts it off, and puts it to work. This is the reason to answer unasked questions: So the answer will exist for future seekers to unbury. Or, put another way, we are responsible for no more than planting the seeds and tending the fields. The harvest will be reaped in God's own time.

CLAIRE BUSHEY, baptized 1980, writer and editor, St. Gertrude Parish in Edgewater.

WELCOME

Blessings for all

What a novel idea it is that we, Catholics, would give input to the selection of a bishop! As I thought about this prospect, I began thinking about the complexities of the city of Chicago and the challenges the archdiocese presents. I thought, too, of the experiences of past generations of both my family and my religious community and their interactions with bishops.

My favorite "bishop story" is one from the last days of my mother's life. Cardinal George had declined to read the book my mother had given him when he first arrived in Chicago, Robert McClory's *Turning Point*, about her experience on the Vatican's birth control commission in the 1960s, and she and he had never really connected in any meaningful way. Yet, he and I had bonded when he publicly supported Deborah's Place, a nonprofit that assists women who were homeless where I was executive director for 13 years. It was during a zoning controversy in the late 1990s over whether to site a transitional housing program in a former parish convent, and the cardinal went out of his way to speak publicly about this issue.

One day in 2005, the cardinal called me to ask about my mother. I invited him to come to visit her. He came, and so did a few others, among them some of her grandchildren. In her final days, my mother's approach to visitors was to ask them to join her in singing children's songs. The cardinal was patient. After a bit, I asked my mother if she would like the cardinal to give her a blessing. After a pregnant pause, she said to me, "Yes, but first I will give him my blessing." Cardinal George graciously deferred to her. This story holds, for me, the seeds of a possible future for our church—one in which women are recognized for who they are as the bearers of many blessings for all.

When I look at our city and consider what it needs in a new pastor, I remember that in the Acts of the Apostles, the daily service to the Christian community was delegated to the deacons, and the apostles took responsibility for prayer and the pastoral care of the people of God. Not much is mentioned about doctrine, and at the time, there was no Vatican in the picture. The bishops I have admired have been pastoral and have prayed well with the people of God.

The Chicago I know best is the city that nurtures grassroots movements, social action, community organizing, and healthy ethnic and cultural diversity. Historically, we are a city with segregated neighborhoods and a strong working class. That is changing, and our leaders, both civic and religious, need to recognize that. We continue to be a city of immigrants and of strong leaders. Of this we remain proud.

We have had a variety of bishops in Chicago. As a Benedictine woman, I suggest that we need a bishop who listens well to both the anguish and the joys of his people, whose approach is both pastoral and collaborative. The healing, inclusive, compassionate approach of Jesus in the Gospels will be key for our next bishop. Chicago is rich in the diversity and giftedness of its people. Called forth in this spirit, we will respond and flourish.

PATRICIA ANN CROWLEY, O.S.B., baptized 1939, former executive director of Howard Area Community Center, Deborah's Place, and the Chicago Continuum of Care, current prioress of Benedictine Sisters of Chicago at St. Scholastica Monastery in Rogers Park.

A church that transforms

It was a December noon, sunny and brisk, and I was a freshman at Loyola University Chicago. Weekday Mass had just let out at our lakefront chapel, Madonna della Strada. I meandered around the lawn outside, thinking about lunch, until a gray-haired woman in her sixties flagged me down. God, I learned, had told her to.

She sat near me at the liturgy, noting my homework on an adjoining chair—a biblical studies book. She sensed God pointing me out. She took her chance.

Reaching into her purse, she produced a cheap, silver-plated Miraculous Medal. Pope John Paul II had blessed it in Rome. She said now I was supposed to have it.

Somewhat befuddled, I started to ask the woman her name. She shook her head: "It's not important. I'm nobody." What was important was the medal, for it would always remind me of something.

"Don't let yourself be pegged," she reported. "Don't let yourself get stuck in a box."

With that, she was done—and so, apparently, was God—and she bid me goodbye. I felt very holy and important. Back in my dorm room I put the medal on a string. I wore it, then I wore it less and less, then I forgot about it.

But the mystery woman turned out to be eerily prophetic. A retiring, pious, by-the-book loner of a freshman, I graduated someone very different: someone who knew and loved many people, someone deeply engaged in my community, and passionate about justice in the world. I did not get pegged or stuck in a box.

Yet I did not turn out that way simply because God gave me magic trinkets. I gradually felt the need to reach out, to search for outlets. I turned to friends, projects, and activities in university ministry. And something very particular, Chicago-style Catholicism, reached back.

Loyola is Jesuit, but it is Chicago Jesuit. The Chicago church is long-famous for its creativity and jagged individuality. In his 1979 book *The Battle for the American Church*, Msgr. George Kelly noted "certain factors uniquely packaged in the Chicago environs: charismatic and overpowering energy in the priestly leadership; educated and classy laity waiting to be motivated for a cause; a good cause at the right time; a freewheeling, independent style of behavior typical of the Windy City itself; and relatively permissive bishops."

I would add that we love a party. And we are quick to embrace outsiders and those who take a long time seeking before they find.

What a church we have in Chicago, a church that transformed me. I pray it may always offer the same to others. I pray the next archbishop of Chicago will, like his predecessors, agree.

JUSTIN SENGSTOCK, baptized 1984, freelance writer and nonprofit employee, Holy Name Cathedral (occasionally) and St. Liborius Parish in Steger.

A different Catholicism

Nuns in Des Moines, where I grew up, taught us to offer our seat on the bus to adults. Their subtext was not, "What is compassionate?" but, "The Protestants see your uniforms: Don't give scandal!"

I found a different Catholicism when I moved to Chicago where we were not other. Even the mayor was Catholic! When the Pope came in 1979, several TV "background" reporters revealed they were Catholic. No Iowa TV anchor would have separated himself from his presumed Protestant viewers by identifying as Catholic.

In Iowa we had built a separate "mission" church for Mexicans in our parish. Many Chicago parishes already had a Spanish Mass, right there in the main church, when I arrived. Chicago masses featured a variety of immigrant faces and races. It seemed very "catholic" to me.

At one Mass a street person took a big gulp from the cup… and then kept guzzling. The Eucharistic Minister tried to stop him, and they struggled for the chalice. I was oddly pleased to belong to a church where homeless alcoholics brought their needs, however inappropriately manifested. My parish also had a Mass for gays. All seemed very "catholic" to me.

When verifying the need of applicants for emergency food and cash where I volunteer, we're instructed: "Try to err on the side of compassion." This interfaith agency seems very "catholic" to me.

A very Chicago Catholic, Joseph Cardinal Bernardin, asked anyone who'd ever been hurt by the church to contact him. He spent the

‹‹ Try to err on the side of compassion. ››

rest of his life replying to those who wrote him, even on his deathbed.

May our leaders understand that whenever our church primarily fears scandal, we sin. May we reflect the cardinal's humility, welcoming *others* to our communion, especially those we've harmed. And when we as church err—as we certainly will—let it be on the side of our Christ-like compassion.

Let us pray to the Lord. Lord, hear our prayer.

Carol DeChant, baptized 1939, writer, wife and grandmother of ten, St. Mary Catholic Church in Evanston.

The world's largest church

For many Catholics, going to Mass every Sunday is the one day a week we practice our faith, think about our Christian beliefs, pray in the sanctuary, and focus on our religion. But a wonderful gift was given to all of us 12 years ago when Relevant Radio began broadcasting.

I had been interviewed on the station a few times in 2007 when my second book, *Parish the Thought*, was published. At that time, I was unable to hear the station in Atlanta. Since moving back to Chicago two years ago, however, anytime I am in the car, most often I will have 950 AM tuned in to listen to Relevant Radio. I appreciate the opportunity to listen to the discussions about various topics in our faith, what the catechism says about various issues, the history of our faith, insights into controversial events, advice from priests, and interviews with Catholics in the working world who bring their faith to their profession. There is so much more, but the main point is that I, and all of us, can practice our faith seven days a week now just by turning on the radio. How often I have felt the Holy Spirit fill me as I listened or prayed along with the radio host. How often I have felt like I am not alone in my faith, listening to so many Catholics share opinions which are in line with our religion.

Often I will be listening at 3 p.m. when radio host Drew Mariani prays the Chaplet of Divine Mercy, and I will join with him. Even though it's a radio station, it is in many ways like being in one of the largest churches in the world, among a community of Christians praying to God. I listen to so many devout and committed Catholics call into the show looking for answers to problems they are facing in their lives. Often I will hear Drew or Father Rocky or Wendy Wiese provide insight or advice that helps those callers, those Catholics, but at the same time helps all of us because many suffer from similar problems or have the same question.

So if you see me driving down I-355 with praying hands holding my steering wheel, you can pretty much guess that I'm in church, praying with Relevant Radio.

JOHN RUANE, baptized 1956, author and journalist, Thirty-Year Husband Club, four children, formerly of St. Bede The Venerable Parish in Scottsdale, now the Catholic Community of St. Jude in New Lenox.

Unity and diversity

Chicago Catholics are a diverse people who shine most brightly when we allow our diversity to form, inform, and stretch us. When all are encouraged to speak, without fear of judgment, we worship in ways that inspire, nurture, and send. We also teach the faith in ways that convert hearts and minds, and serve the poor through gospel justice and charity.

I have been blessed to serve as pastor of two active, engaged, and faithful parishes. Both embrace diverse cultures, religious traditions, and languages of worship. Those of more traditional backgrounds and those envisioning new ways to be a church strive to hear one another and respect the importance of the gifts of each and all. Yet many fear that the very creativity that brings life to the parish is threatened by an institutional trend toward a uniformity that harshly judges whatever does not conform.

I hope that you will embrace our unity *and* our diversity so that both may bear fruit. I pray that you will reawaken the great Chicago tradition of creative initiatives in worship, formation, justice, and charity. Many initiatives now stay at the parish level for fear they will die on the vine or be uprooted if shared with the larger church.

Three years ago, St. Nicholas parishioners doubted that a parish conversation on women deacons would be tolerated and colleagues expressed similar concerns. Yet we developed a rich dialogue among parishioners and with Cardinal Francis George. On the other hand, I hesitate to discuss what makes Sunday liturgy at St. Nicholas so vibrant. We worship within the Catholic liturgical tradition. Yet sharing the specifics might invite a confrontation with a liturgical legalism that equates universality with uniformity and inhibits appropriately diverse liturgical expression.

I pray for an apostle who will lead us into a vibrant future in

Christ and for God's people. I pray also that as you come to know us, you will come to love us. I hope you can affirm the good that you see in us while challenging us to go further. I ask you to encourage us to respond creatively to our challenges, to deepen in us that which is essential to our unity, and to call us to flourish in our diversity.

REV. WILLIAM TKACHUK, baptized 1955, pastor of St. Nicholas Church in Evanston.

Pastoring the flock

My life has been blessed by two pastors who have taken joy in their flocks, in the creativity, energy, and particular spirituality of the people in the pews.

Father Robert Oldershaw, a holy and gifted man, said once in reference to ministering Communion: "Get out of the way, and let God be God." He also addressed the conflicting beliefs and preferences of our diverse parish: "We're all family here, and like families, we don't always agree." These words, devoid of "should's" and "shalt not's," gave parishioners space to explore and to fly with the Holy Spirit. Under his watch we learned to create liturgies that supported and nurtured our linguistically and ethnically diverse parish, to build new bridges, and to take our beliefs out of the church building and into new arenas where we work for justice and peace, in large ways and in small.

Our current pastor, Father Bill Tkachuk, is clearly energized rather than threatened by the empowered flock he greeted upon coming to St. Nick's in Evanston. He has encouraged discourse between folks who disagree on issues like funding the parish school or working toward ordaining a woman deacon. He has welcomed the work of the parish's gay and lesbian group and is comfortable discussing women's ordination. He ensures that discussions remain civil and respectful, and that when a specific decision is needed, it is one everyone can live with.

‹‹ Like families, we don't always agree. ››

Good pastors know that the real work comes from the pews, and they rejoice in the wisdom and investment of the people they shepherd. Our church should always be a work in progress, responding to the needs of our time and place while remaining faithful to the gospel. This inclusive vision, and above all the joy in others' wisdom and understanding of the Spirit Sophia, is what I look for in a bishop.

Julie Drew, baptized 1953, teacher, placement aide at the Oakton College ESL program, St. Nicholas Church in Evanston.

Where two or more are gathered

Most Sundays, I take my elderly mother to Mass at Ascension Church in Oak Park, a large, vibrant community of roughly 2,500 families. I was baptized there 60 years ago this June. My parents had to choose between St. Catherine of Siena and Ascension. I was the third child. (Eventually there were six, all boys.) My dad learned that Ascension School had just built a new gym with a beautiful parquet floor. We went to Ascension.

So our roots run deep. I enjoy taking my mom to church because it helps her stay connected. We sit up front because she's 86. The first pew provides real immediacy. Sometimes a little too much. Frankly, many Sundays are a struggle for me. I'm a writer, editor, and critic. It's my profession and my nature. Sitting through the Liturgy of the Word and the preparation for the Eucharist makes me want to subject this ritual to a rigorous rewrite—and that was before the "new translation." Now I wince as my fellow parishioners gamely say "consubstantial" and "He was incarnate of the Blessed Virgin"—tone-deaf, leaden language from bureaucrats in love with Latin derivatives. It holds us at a distance.

Then there's the Nicene Creed. Christianity, when you break it down to essentials, is elegantly simple. It centers on love, both of God and our fellow humans. The more removed we are from these essentials, the more trouble we get into. The hierarchy has gotten into lots of trouble. What does it say about the Catholic Church when the word "love" fails to appear in either version of our creed?

It says we need to refocus.

But just when I'm about to despair, a remarkable thing happens. People leave the pews and head toward the altar, a long procession, single file, accompanied by music. Some literally believe they are receiving the body and blood of Jesus Christ. Some believe this as a beautiful metaphor. Some simply receive a circle of unleavened bread and a sip of sweet wine. Somehow it all produces the same result.

I have a ringside seat for this remarkable parade of humanity, dazzlingly diverse in body type and fashion sense, their demeanor a reflection of lives joyfully and painfully lived. I know some of their histories, their struggles, their setbacks, and accomplishments. But in all, you sense the goodness. There are families with small children, looking up in awe at the priest or communion ministers, who smile and put a hand on their heads or shoulders. There are adolescents looking painfully self-conscious. There are elders, bent and battling their bodies.

Some exchange a few words with the pastor. Some look sleepy, some indifferent, some thoughtful, some happy, some not. They represent the full spectrum of understanding, feeling, and belief. Each is a vast ocean of consciousness, a complex mystery. Each has an odyssey worth telling. It reminds me that Jesus the God/man never wrote anything down. He attracted a small group of disciples, imparted his wisdom, then left it up to them.

He left it up to them. Talk about an act of faith.

It could have been anyone.

It could have been us.

Something happens each Sunday as this ragtag confederacy of isolates is transformed into a "people," the people of God, what Vatican II defined as "church." I realize anew, with the freshness of epiphany, that communion isn't host and wine, body and blood, bells

‹‹ Each has an odyssey worth telling. ››

and smells, hymns and prayers. Communion is the shared experience of communal union, which happens whenever two or more are gathered in God's name. The Spirit inhabits the space between us until there is no space at all.

What am I looking for in the next archbishop? Someone who has experienced this—who recognizes that Catholics are all over the map and doesn't lose sleep over it, who doesn't demand doctrinal correctness or obedience oaths. I want someone who is deeply moved when this procession shuffles toward him each Sunday.

KEN TRAINOR, baptized 1952, community journalist, author, lifelong Oak Park resident, Ascension Catholic Church in Oak Park.

Unique and creative Chicago

Imagine this sight: We are in Holy Name Cathedral. Cardinal Joseph Bernardin's body, Chicago's archbishop, lays in state after his death from cancer. His body is in the center of the cathedral, just under the steps leading to the altar below a large and impressive crucifix. Below the cross stand three rabbis. They lead the congregation in an interfaith remembrance of someone they knew and came to love. It is an extraordinary experience that reflects an extraordinary man's life, as well as an extraordinary city.

Chicago is unique in Catholic history. Cardinal Bernardin was able to unite and embrace the entire city, Catholic and non-Catholic alike, and reflect to the city its best self. The church of Chicago, at its best, has been the seedbed of great creativity for the U.S. church and for the nation. That creativity has expressed itself in many ways. One can point to the birth of the Catholic Youth Organization (CYO), the best known and most extensive youth outreach in U.S. Catholicism, and the diffusion of Catholic Action from here throughout the nation, including the Christian Family Movement, which engages families with the gospel and through it, the issues of society.

There is also a liturgical richness exemplified by the Office for Divine Worship, which helps the diocese and parishes with their liturgical training needs, and the nonprofit Liturgy Training Publications, which has created numerous and diverse publications related to liturgy for Catholics worldwide. A strong social justice focus has

‹‹ **A strong social justice focus has flourished.** ››

flourished here too, manifested in the work of Msgr. Jack Egan in urban ministry, the development of young adult ministry, and parishes with great impact on our city and its people, such as Old St. Patrick's.

This emphasis on justice and creativity has expanded beyond the Chicago church to the secular world. For example, an influential international movement began with women who belonged to the Christian Family Movement. They met in Franklin Park, part of metropolitan Chicago. They saw a need at a time when breastfeeding was discouraged, judged it to be significant, and founded the organization that became La Leche League, which promotes breastfeeding. It is now in 68 countries.

Will this rich tradition of creativity, social engagement, and impact on our world continue? Can the Catholic Church of Chicago continue to call forth and develop the creativity and structures that meet the pressing needs of the 21st century?

JUAN LORENZO HINOJOSA, spiritual theologian and founder of Solidarity Bridge, baptized in 1946, husband and father of five, St. Nicholas Church in Evanston.

Acts 2:5-13 revisited

Pentecost is never ordinary at St. Gertrude Parish. We celebrate a combined liturgy bringing the diversity of three Masses together in one. The church is full to overflowing. The energy is palpable. 2012 being the centennial of the parish made this year's Pentecost liturgy memorable. Instead of presenting our annual Spirit award to individuals or parish organizations (as is our tradition), the decision was made to recognize all our parishioners decade by decade. We began by asking those whose families had belonged to the parish from the start—100 years ago—to stand. The applause was spontaneous. They remained standing as those here 90 years were then recognized. More applause. So it continued until our most recent parishioners stood with the entire congregation. There was sustained applause for one another and those who had preceded us.

I was privileged to see not only faces but the stories of the hearts behind the faces. Here was the old-timer whose wife was battling Alzheimer's. Behind them were the two I married five years ago trying so hard to have a child. Next to them was a lesbian couple; one of the women's grandfather had thanked me in tears for the child's baptism two years ago. A student from Loyola University who later told me he was entering the Jesuit novitiate sat with other young adults from the parish. I saw people with whom I had grieved and children to whom I had given their First Holy Communion. Parishioners prayed with Polish, Spanish, Vietnamese, Tagalong, Italian, and other accents. There were Iraqi refugees and retired professionals, religious sisters from many communities, priests no longer active in ministry, Jesuit lay volunteers, and people born in County Mayo in Ireland. Lifelong Catholics sat next to those who had completed the R.C.I.A. at Easter and danced the tarantella with me around the church at Easter vigil in celebration of God's courtship. A woman completing a degree at

29

the Catholic Theological Union shared the sign of peace with an anti-war activist. A parent patiently cleaned up the Cheerios her son had dumped out of his sippy cup.

Some are secure in their faith. Others have been hurt by actions less than pastoral that have plagued the church. Many know people who have left the church and wonder why they are staying. But at this moment in our history, as everyone comes forward, hands outstretched, to be anointed with oil, the Spirit is moving, urging and nudging St. Gertrude's into its second hundred years. May our new archbishop be led by that same Spirit.

REV. DOMINIC GRASSI, baptized 1947, priest, author, speaker, pastor at St. Gertrude Parish in Edgewater.

Living the Gospel

I was born and raised a Catholic in Hawaii. Learned the Baltimore Catechism, the Latin Mass, and various religious practices—I learned very well. I stopped practicing in Catholic middle school and high school, except enough to get by. Still, the Marianist brothers who taught at my high school encouraged me to join the religious life; I chose to remain in the lay life. My discovery of existential literature and the convening of Vatican II led to a whole new world. Discomforting concepts and feelings I had been experiencing but unable to verbalize were beginning to be addressed.

Vatican II introduced the notion of the church as the People of God, that there is a critical role for the laity in the church, and that the church has an essential role to play in the modern world. I was fortunate to attend a Catholic university—Gonzaga. There I was able to learn to put into practice Vatican II teachings. We are all part of the People of God. We each have a role in co-creating the world. We must play an active role to bring the world to fulfillment.

Vatican II was my primary motivation in returning to the church. At parishes in Spokane, Washington, Evanston, Illinois, Fort Hood and Belton, Texas, and in Arlington Heights, I participated in various aspects of church life. I selected prayers and readings for my own wedding and for the baptism of my children. I drafted prayers, read at Mass, and sang in the choir. I studied scripture and theology, did catechetical work, and developed my parish's marriage preparation program. I worked at two homeless shelters, gave rides to AIDS patients, and visited seniors in nursing homes.

I grew up in the tradition of the Baltimore Catechism—memorize, not study or reflect. I was very good at this, but gradually, dissatisfied. I do not accept change easily, but need time to reflect and pray. I accept change when it makes sense to me; Vatican II did. I was awakened to the need to grow with, not to fear, the presence of the Spirit with us, not to be happy with our lot, but to shoulder our responsibility to help everyone grow to full personhood. Pre-Vatican II demanded that we say our prayers and obey rules. Vatican II taught me that that was not enough. We are not here to be passive followers, but to actively live out the gospel.

We are not simply individuals, rather others contribute to our understanding of God. The diversity of Hawaii and Chicago expressed concretely the richness of God. We try to further express this richness in our thinking, our religious practices, our approaches to address the needs of people. We must not fear difference, but welcome and learn from it, because each part contributes more and more to the fuller grasp of God and our role in creation.

RICHARD FUNG, baptized 1945, retired, husband, grandfather, St. James Parish in Arlington Heights.

The people's bishop

Jack Egan was a people's priest and, some in Chicago say, the "people's bishop." He lived Vatican II before it ever happened, believing in and empowering the laity as full disciples; performing Catholic social teaching in specific projects to support worker rights, racial equality, economic justice, and women in the church; befriending and collaborating with religious leaders from all denominations and traditions; and speaking with courage and prophetic eloquence to bishops. Chicago loved Jack and drew from his deep faith. His message was more than "God *loves* you"—more like, "God *needs* you!" The reply of many was an effort to become and to live our best selves: more generous, more understanding, more humble, more willing to do justice.

I got to know and love Jack in 1989 when I became director of university ministry at DePaul University, where he held the title of "special assistant to the president." In addition to his wry sense of humor and his respectful, gentlemanly presence, I found him to be not only knowledgeable, but wise. He saw deeply and evoked an alert awareness. You were never just in the room with Jack—you were engaged in a personal dynamic that felt both affirming and challenging. He had a genuine humility. Never arrogant or "above" you, he was simply himself.

Jack really got the Gospel of Jesus Christ. Somewhere along the line, he must have eaten it. He never used it to judge others or as a weapon for coercion, never tried to manipulate some kind of false piety or compliance. He knew that this was Good News—liberating and life-giving news, a stunning affirmation of the human project that worked its dynamic in real people. He knew that behind every face was a story—a drama of hope and tragedy, folly and tenderness, a hunger to be found and loved. This Good News could never be reduced to rules to be complied with or doctrine to be memorized and spoken. The Gospel was God's loving embrace of human beings and a call to become that loving embrace for others in real and pragmatic ways. When he preached, his words were the real expression of real faith, a real invitation to follow the Lord. But mostly Jack preached with relationships and action: being with others, affirming others, challenging others, calling others forth for service and justice.

Toward the end of his life (he died in 2001), Jack was dismayed by ecclesial intransigence, concerned that its social teaching was losing its credibility in the seeming inability of church leadership to apply it within the church itself. In a speech at "The First Friday Club," he used the fog off Lake Michigan and the Chicago skyline as a metaphor—you knew the Holy Spirit was there in the church, but you could barely see it. Jack never lost faith. He was a Chicago gem!

ROBERT LUDWIG, baptized 1944, author, theologian, university professor, husband and father of three adult children, St. Nicholas Church in Evanston.

A Body broken and renewed

Barely having passed through the preteen years, I asserted to my choir boy father that I was no longer going to Mass. I had tasted and seen the goodness of the Lord at a summer camp that watered the dying seeds of faith within me. That camp was not Catholic. No Catholic I knew raised up holy hands in worship or name-dropped Jesus without uttering his last name, Christ. The volatile high school years passed as I sought God at different churches while my family headed to the church of my upbringing without me. It would be another two years in college—a Catholic one, in fact—before I returned to the one, holy, Catholic, and apostolic church.

Take this, all of you, and eat it: This is my Body which will be given up for you.

Those five years of voluntary abstinence from the Body produced a drought in my soul in which the foundation dried out and cracked. I longed for the living waters of the Word made flesh to commission a deluge, a washing away of the shackles of human-instituted patriarchy and exclusionary doctrine that marred my thirst for a life reborn in Christ. But God promised to never send another flood.

Take this, all of you, and drink from it: This is the cup of my Blood, the Blood of the new and everlasting covenant.

Stricken with frailty after all these years, I crawled through yet more churches with more egalitarian flavors, aching for my sisters to have a deeper seat at the table. But I only stumbled upon different rules, not the radical love of Jesus shining forth from our birthright as sons and daughters of the Almighty One. I tripped over the ornate robes of the hierarchies ruled and defined by the more privileged half of the population. I did not find the ruins of the temple—those monuments to prideful systems of power over empowerment—that Jesus said he'd topple in three days because he is the only true king. The peppery incense of defeat began to suffocate me again.

It will be shed for you and for all so that sins may be forgiven.

But then, *behold!* A slight prompting, a whisper, that dared me to commit to Mass for the forty days of Lent. It was just a few of us, huddled around the table with tired eyes from late nights of studying. We linked hands as we prayed the Our Father. We lifted up our burdens and blessings in petitions. But when it came time to partake in the holy mystery of water and wine, of Body and Blood, of Jesus Christ and everlasting life, I crossed my chest and bowed my head.

Night after night passed in the shadowy chapel, our own upper room celebrating the Last Supper. The ritual seeped into my veins, my heart, my lungs. A suppleness flowed through me as my lungs inhaled, slowly and then deeply, the fresh aroma of the Spirit. And from this Lenten promise, from the ashes of Ash Wednesday to the hope of the resurrection, I was reborn in the faith of my birth.

Do this in memory of me.

As members of the universal church, we are this Body, intended for acting justly, loving mercy, and walking humbly with our God. When we break the bread and drink from the cup and feed the hungry and break from the strongholds of patriarchy, let us do this in memory of the one who was broken first. May we as *imago dei*, God in us, experience *Emmanuel*, God with us.

DANIELLE LOVALLO VERMEER, baptized 1989, consultant, writer, wife, St. Josaphat Parish in Lincoln Park and Vineyard Christian Fellowship.

A muscular faith

One of the pope's many titles is Servant of the Servants of God, an allusion to Jesus' model of leading through service. While it doesn't always feel like the church hierarchy leads this way, I know someone who does: Sister Christina Fuller, the director of religious education at St. Nicholas in Evanston.

After graduating from Quigley Prep Seminary North in 1967, I was, as my godmother likes to say, a "roamin' Catholic." I became active in social justice issues, but unlike others in my family, not within the context of the church. I dropped out of the University of Chicago to participate in the student protest movement; eventually, I became a conscientious objector to the Vietnam War. Over the next two decades I joined the fights against apartheid in South Africa and the United States' support for dictatorships in Latin America, as well as working for racial equality and workers' rights here at home. But my faith was dormant.

One of the key people who brought me back home to the church was Sister Christina. My father, a longtime parishioner at St. Nick's, had died from a brain tumor, and I had stopped by the rectory to handle some of the arrangements for his funeral. I met Sister Christina as I was leaving.

"How come we don't see you at St. Nick's?" she asked. I was somewhat taken aback. Sister Christina isn't afraid to call people out. It's why she's so good at recruiting volunteers for parish ministries. I

‹‹ **Sister Christina isn't afraid to call people out.** ››

told her I was too unsure in my faith.

"Come on," she responded. "Faith is like a muscle that you have to exercise. You have to work at it!"

Her words pushed me to take my search for meaning in a new direction. Her example—this woman is a dynamo, involved in so many parish activities even as she nourishes and develops the faith of our children—was one of the main elements compelling me to take that step back to the community, to share in the Eucharistic celebration, to work at re-establishing as a core element in my life and thinking the message of God's love.

I want to see our entire church be as vibrant as the parish I am part of. I think there are many other roamin' Catholics who could be drawn back into more active participation in our communion. Servant leaders: Sister Christina embodies this ideal, and it is what our church and our archdiocese needs.

DAMIAN BARTA, baptized 1949, son of Bernice and Russell Barta, building manager for 20 years, married to Barbara, father to Morgan and Andy, St. Nicholas Church in Evanston.

A spiritual home

It's easy to miss Immaculate Conception Church in Old Town. There is no steeple, no bell tower, no stained glass windows. The original church burned in the Great Chicago Fire. Lightning damaged the rebuilt church, and it eventually was razed. The sanctuary moved to the basement of the parish school. To this day, Immaculate Conception is a parish without a traditional church building. But for me, it will always be the epitome of a spiritual home.

I first heard of Immaculate Conception as a young journalist new to Chicago. Its pastor, Father Patrick Lee, celebrated a 4 p.m. Mass on Saturdays in the party room of the Sandburg Village condominium complex near where I lived. A church that was willing to go to the people rather than the other way around was one I wanted to know more about. I had heard about Fat Pat's moving homilies. The first time I listened to one, I wasn't disappointed. He spoke of the importance of symbols and rituals, and how clever Jesus was to ask his followers to remember him through the ordinary table items of bread and wine. He told of going to the cemetery every year on the anniversary of his father's death, lighting up a cigar and placing it on the edge of the gravestone as he watched memories of his father form in the smoke. By the time he was finished, there wasn't a dry eye in room, either for his father or for Jesus.

The writer John Shea offers one of the best definitions of *parish*: "Here comes everybody." At Immaculate Conception, Harry, the homeless man who slept through Sunday Masses in a back pew, sat alongside Helene Curtis Inc. president Ron Gidwitz and his family at coffee and doughnuts afterward. As a single person with no nearby family, I never had to worry about where to spend holidays. Friends from Immaculate Conception invited me. When I suddenly was laid off by the *Wall Street Journal* while working in its London bureau, only a year after being a finalist for the Pulitzer Prize, a couple from Immaculate Conception let me stay at their home until I got sorted out, even though the husband in the family had recently lost *his* job.

Father Pat thrived on being a shepherd to his parishioners. He sensed that I felt lost and dejected after my layoff. He invited me to accompany him on visits to the sick and homebound. I will always remember a visit he made to a man dying of AIDS. The disease had so ravaged the man's body he was virtually consumed by the king-size bed where he lay. To give him communion, Father Pat had to climb on the bed and approach the man on his knees. Later he said, "That's the way we should always approach the dying, on our knees."

Gratitude is something I gained at Immaculate Conception. I have since married and moved to central Illinois. But I have never found another parish like Immaculate Conception. No matter where I live, it will always be my parish. Here comes everybody.

Judith Valente, author, poet and journalist, formerly of Immaculate Conception in Old Town.

STRUGGLE

On loving and leaving

I was sitting on the steps of the U.S. Capitol, facing the Washington Monument, watching a vibrant sunset, surrounded by 19 other fellows who'd just completed a weeklong orientation at the Congressional Hunger Center (CHC), a nonprofit that trains individuals to advocate for anti-hunger policies. Our leaders had brought us to this place to stand before our peers and say what motivated us to choose to dedicate a year of our lives to social justice work.

For a secular group, the exercise felt surprisingly religious in nature. We were going "as the spirit led us"—my words, not theirs—so I had a chance to hear some inspiring stories before I stood to "testify," unsure of what I would say.

"It's faith," I said, surprising myself.

I grew up a Black Catholic in the metro Atlanta area, where "religious" was a term reserved for zealous Christian evangelists who wore their faith on their sleeves. It was questionable whether Catholics were even Christian. I never felt religious at all. Yet I went to church religiously every Sunday and participated in my parish during college. Prayer was a central part of my family life.

I detailed for my cohort how I had a plan that fell apart, only to receive an e-mail about the CHC's fellowship program, and how I was sure, because of the way everything had lined up, it was God. How I had a faith that put social justice at the forefront. I told them about the Beatitudes, Romero's martyrdom, the U.S. Conference of Catholic Bishops' pastoral letter "Economic Justice for All." Finally, I told them how I did not want work that was separate from the social justice my faith called me to. It was a powerful moment for me.

Five years later I still feel the same passion for the church's social justice teachings; unfortunately, it feels less and less at the forefront for the institutional church. I increasingly find myself distinguishing between the faith that I was raised in and the institution that has different priorities.

In that moment on the Capitol steps, I unabashedly embraced my church. Lately I've felt like that same church, which I love, is forcefully pushing me away. The beauty of the Catholic church is the universal. There has always been a home for me, a progressive Catholic, despite the fact that I speak a different language than my conservative counterparts. Now I hear mounting cries saying, "If you don't like it, leave."

I cannot imagine leaving the church that brought me my worldview, my compass, the church that is my rock. I hope the next cardinal makes me once again feel welcome at home, in my archdiocese of this beautiful, universal church.

ADRIENNE ALEXANDER, baptized 1986, union lobbyist and policy researcher, San Pío V Parish in Pilsen.

Do-it-yourself excommunication

For more than 60 years I was a practicing Catholic. This was first in Iowa, where I grew up, then in Chicago where I graduated from and worked for a Catholic university. It was there I met Henry J. Lambin, psychologist, loving father and husband and lifelong Catholic. Over the years I was an active member of St. Gertrude's and then St. Ita's. And I was, for about a year, a member of the Archdiocesan Pastoral Council. Yet I am now a member of Immanuel Evangelical Lutheran Church.

What happened was this. Each member of the Archdiocesan Pastoral Council served on a committee. I asked for and was appointed to the social justice committee. That was the beginning of what unexpectedly became the end. I questioned how the prophetic voice of the church was being raised, particularly in regards to divorced Catholics and to our gay and lesbian brothers and sisters. Eventually I concluded I could no longer represent a traditional Catholic position. Because when I think of these issues, I think, what if the divorced person were my child? What if the LGBT person were my child? Because it is always someone's child.

I wrote a letter of resignation to the cardinal, out of respect for him and his position, stating why I was resigning and moving on to pursue other Christian spiritual paths. While the church spoke prophetically on some social justice issues, on others, its voice was misguided.

"[The church] will not allow divorced Catholics to remarry, yet will grant annulments when a marriage has existed for years, and with children," I wrote. "It does not accept long-term committed relationships among lesbians and homosexuals, yet affirms the sanctity of marriage. ... I am a straight, gray-haired granny ...(who) was lucky enough to have a wonderful husband. ... But the gays and lesbians, these are also my brothers and sisters, some surely more spiritual and selfless than I. And had I been less lucky in my marriage, the divorced woman in the pew could have been me."

So began my pilgrimage.

Shortly after, I sent a copy of this letter to Joe Murray, the head of the Chicago Rainbow Sash Movement, because of the LGBT concerns in it. Rainbow Sash is an LGBT organization that advocates for the church to change its teachings on homosexuality. I had received a form postcard from an assistant to the cardinal, but nothing else— that is, until Joe Murray asked to circulate the letter on the Rainbow Sash website. He explained there is a high suicide rate among young gay men and that my letter would represent a kind of affirmation from the mainstream. I said yes. I sent a second letter to the cardinal to inform him of how and why the letter would be circulated, so he wouldn't be taken by surprise. Then things suddenly became ... lively.

First I received a request from an assistant to the cardinal to send a copy of the first letter, which had either gone missing or was possibly in the cardinal's mailbag on the way to Rome. I did. The cardinal, I was told, would respond on his return from a trip to Rome. He did. The response was a letter from the cardinal, enclosing a copy of a typewritten form called: "REQUEST TO LEAVE THE CATHOLIC CHURCH BY A FORMAL ACT." It appeared the form hadn't been used in some time since the typeface indicated it had been typed on a typewriter and then photocopied. According to the instructions, the form was to be signed and notarized, then returned to the Office of the Chancellor.

I think the form was misnamed. This was not a request. It was a "Do-It-Yourself Excommunication" form. It sternly warned me that I could not receive the sacraments in a Catholic church. I have, as I have always had, respect for the sacraments. To agree not to receive them again would be wholly dishonest. From my perspective, it is the

Table of the Lord, not one with a card: "Reserved for Members Only." The form also warned me that I could not have Catholic burial rites. My husband is buried at St. Boniface in the Lambin family plot. Someday I intended to be buried beside him. And yes, there is room for me in the family plot, Protestant or not. I know, I checked. The dead are sometimes more open-minded than the living. I didn't sign it.

I did, however, continue my pilgrimage. In April 2005 I joined Immanuel Evangelical Lutheran Church in Chicago, and have remained there ever since. (Yes, I let them know the above story, so they knew what they were getting.) I have done a lot of thinking in the years since I received that form. And I have come to feel more and more strongly, not less so, about all of these issues of justice and full inclusion for all God's children: for our LGBT brothers and sisters, our divorced and remarried ones, and women who feel called to the priesthood.

Do I miss being Catholic, after being part of the church for so many years? Yes. There were many things I loved about Catholic spirituality and culture. Breaking up is hard to do. Does my present faith community at Immanuel have meaning for me, in terms of worship, spirituality, social justice, and community? Yes, it does. I am grateful. And I'm still learning. Once a pilgrim ....

HELEN REICHERT LAMBIN, baptized 1934, author, retired university program coordinator, widow of Henry J. Lambin, mother of three, Immanuel Evangelical Lutheran Church in Edgewater, Evangelical Lutheran Church in America.

The person inside

We just had a death in Chicago's Catholic Native American community, an elder who was transgendered. When I got news of her passing, I was relieved and saddened. I was relieved because she did not have to suffer any more health problems or continue to deal with the pain of not being accepted by others. Saddened because she was my friend.

When I first met "Vanessa"—not her real name— she was sitting at the table in the gathering room at Kateri Center, the archdiocese's ministry to Native American Catholics. When she found out that I was Native and in discernment for the priesthood, she became excited. There are a number of priests across the country who minister to Native Americans, but few come from their ranks. After a couple of conversations, we became friends. A visit to the center wasn't complete unless we had a chance to chat. We celebrated Thanksgiving together with the other seminarians at our community house.

Some people just click, and Vanessa and I were that way.

During our two-year friendship, other people at the center kept warning me to stay away from Vanessa. She was a troublemaker and "not right in the head," they said. I ignored them. As I got to know Vanessa more, I learned that she left her Minnesota hometown early in life because she was an outcast. Heartbreakingly, she still was. I always asked her why, and she said "personality differences."

Vanessa had some heart problems, and I always thought that

‹‹ Heartbreakingly, she still was an outcast. ››

was the reason she looked the way she did. She was balding, her voice was feminine with a hint of masculinity, and her hands were big for a woman. I never questioned her about any of these things.

It wasn't until she got really ill and some friends went to see her that I learned that Vanessa had the body of a man, though she'd lived as a woman for decades. I was shocked, but I never let that affect the way I thought of her. She was a good, practicing Catholic. She met the cardinal numerous times and had a plethora of friends who were priests. They all knew and saw Vanessa, the person on the inside. It would be nice if the next archbishop had the same grace as the people who knew my friend: the gift of seeing the interior of people and using that to build up the Kingdom of God.

MICHEAL JOHN RESZLER, baptized 1989, Native American from Bad River Band of Lake Superior Chippewa, administrative assistant, Kateri Center of Chicago in North Center.

Blessed are the peacemakers

Eight years ago I moved from an affluent neighborhood on Chicago's North Side to Back of the Yards—once the home of the mighty Union Stockyards, now a humble, hardworking neighborhood of Mexican immigrants and African-Americans. Unfortunately, many Chicagoans only know Back of the Yards from news reports of gang-related shootings and deaths.

One of my first friends on my new block was 10-year-old Daniel, a quiet boy with dark, thoughtful eyes who lived across the street. Together we read *The Curious Incident of the Dog in the Night-Time*, a difficult novel I wouldn't have tried with any other neighbor kid. We made pizza. We played four-square on my parking pad. Daniel went to the local parish, St. Joseph's, for catechism every Saturday morning.

In eighth grade Daniel was accepted to a good high school. I thought his future would be OK. I was looking forward to helping him with high school essays, college applications, and finding scholarships.

His freshman year, his older brother was shot and killed. That's when everything changed for Daniel. The one high school essay I helped him revise was about his brother's death and funeral. After that, he began to disappear. He would wave from across the street but not stop to talk. The artistic graffiti he liked to draw turned into gang graffiti. Once, at dusk, I called him over to talk in front of my house. A police car coming up the street flashed a spotlight on us.

Last summer he told me his high school had kicked him out, and he was returning to our neighborhood school for senior year. The last time I saw him was the second day of school in August 2011, when we talked for a bit on the corner right after school ended. That day a drive-by shooting took place, and he was arrested because someone said he was in the car. He is still awaiting trial. I am an alibi witness because he was with me during part of the time in question. Though I believe he was not part of this shooting, I don't know what other acts of violence he may have been part of. I hear from friends that he is ready to make a change in his life when he returns to life on the outside. I pray that may happen.

Here in our neighborhood, Holy Cross/IHM Parish and Precious Blood Ministry of Reconciliation are known in both Catholic and city circles for their work helping young people look beyond gang life. Cardinal George has lent his support to CeaseFire, an effort to change the mindset about violence both in neighborhoods and in the criminal justice system. But all this good work has yet to reach Daniel. Can the church in Chicago extend its role and reach as a peacemaker, so that one day our city will not lead the nation in youth lost to violence? I pray that may happen.

MAUREEN KELLEHER, baptized 1967, writer, wife, mother, friend of the Catholic Worker, Holy Cross/Immaculate Heart of Mary Parish in Back of the Yards.

Questions and answers

As a young, single laywoman, graduate school at a Catholic seminary was challenging. Perhaps never more so than the semester I took "Sexual Ethics" with 20 seminarians. That class was a perfect storm for controversy—challenging course material; a variety of personal feelings and experiences; sometimes clear, sometimes murky, always passionate directives from the church.

Despite the controversy, what has stayed with me is the anxiety I felt from my seminarian classmates. It was often clear that they weren't invested in the intellectual gray area, and they weren't looking to prepare for contentious dialogue on tough issues; they were worried about having the answers for whatever questions future parishioners might approach them with.

I don't blame them for that, and I don't envy them. I think few things in the world are more difficult than being a confessor. But I also worry about their approach. How many parishioners are going to come to these men looking for prescriptions for the issues we covered? The church's teachings on many common sexual issues are clear, whether or not parishioners accept them. More importantly, will having "an answer" serve these future priests better than knowing how to accompany those who do approach them through the discernment process?

One short year after finishing that ethics class, I found myself in a different but equally challenging situation: I was surrounded by several bright, faithful students, eating ice cream in the coffee shop at the small, Catholic college where I now work. We had just finished a leader meeting for an upcoming retreat they were working hard to prepare. As it often does with college kids, the subject of sex had come up, and I found myself being asked a lot of questions about what the church expects young adults to do in their personal relationships.

"So, what's the answer?" a particularly smart and conservative junior asked me when the conversation turned to public health concerns. "Just give everyone condoms?!"

He wasn't interested in a simple answer—a lifelong Catholic discerning his own religious vocation, I knew that he knew and believed in the church's teachings on condom use. As is true with most of the young adults I work with and their questions about the church's teachings, this student's question belied a hunger to participate in discussion, to have the question reflected back to him, to be invited into the decision-making process of what is good and right in his life.

The anxious seminarians from my ethics class represent, I believe, the current misguided approach of the church to helping young adults form their moral decision-making process: Give directives, have answers to every question, limit discussion, and limit dissent. We stunt the potential participation of passionate young Catholics by showing them so little trust; they have questions, but they want to be a part of discovering the answers. We need a church leader to engage young Catholics, encourage their participation in dialogue, and build the trust that breeds love.

CLAIRE MARKHAM, baptized 1985, writer, ethicist, campus minister, Old St Patrick's Church in the West Loop.

‹‹ He wasn't interested in a simple answer. ››

'They took my church away from me'

I arrived at the suburban Chicago hospital where I work as a chaplain on a January morning expecting a fairly typical day. Not uncommonly, I began the day by visiting a patient who requested that a chaplain see him before his knee surgery.

I had no idea I was about to have one of the most moving conversations of my life.

I was warmly welcomed by a calm, jovial man in his mid-70s, with slightly graying hair and a beautiful smile. We chatted for a few minutes, and I was charmed by his Irish brogue and sweet personality. His surgery time was fast approaching, so I asked him if he wanted to receive communion while in the hospital. Tears began to fall. I sat for a minute holding his hand before telling him I was sorry to bring up an apparently difficult topic before surgery. He waved off my apology as he wiped away a few more tears.

Then he explained why he was so heartbroken. He said he had always been a good and faithful Catholic. But he had stopped going to Mass two years ago because he was so bothered by the hierarchy's handling of the sexual abuse crisis.

He grabbed my hand and cried, "They took my church away from me."

My heart couldn't help but break a little too. Together, we grieved for the loss of faith in our community of faith. Then we prayed for his surgery and recovery, but also for his healing beyond, and for our church to be reconciled unto itself.

He told me he ran into his priest recently, and the priest asked him why he was not attending church anymore. My patient told his pastor the pain he felt about the hierarchy's actions. And the priest turned and walked away without uttering one word in response.

When I think about what I would like to see in Chicago's next archbishop, I think of my patient. He represents for me the many Catholics who feel grief over what has happened in their church and the crimes committed by their trusted leaders. I want to see an archbishop with honesty, realism, and humility, who will address the pain and confusion our church members feel. I want to hear someone say, "No, we will not deflect away from these important issues. We have work to do and healing to seek."

My patient's church will never be the same again. But I pray for someone who will lead us in the delicate work of putting this church back together again. That takes acknowledging what has been broken. I am so thankful to this man, whose grief exposed to me my own. We found a moment of healing grace together, not surprisingly, by being in communion with one another.

LAUREN IVORY, baptized in 1979, hospital chaplain, Old St. Patrick's Church in the West Loop and a small faith-sharing group.

A kind of martyrdom

In 2010 Janine Denomme died of cancer. We were members of the St. Gertrude parish in Edgewater. We served on the parish council together. Janine was one of the pillars of the parish.

But, when she died, we couldn't host her funeral.

The archdiocese said she couldn't be buried out of any Catholic church—because, a month earlier, Janine had been ordained a priest by the Roman Catholic Womenpriests organization.

Janine loved the church, even though, as a lesbian, she argued with some Catholic teachings. She sought priesthood to be even more closely involved in the church's mission.

Women would make great priests. Just look at the deeply spiritual, vibrantly active female pastors in other Christian faiths as well as the women serving as rabbis. Just look at the women doctors, public officials, firefighters, college professors, judges, editors, CEOs, and cops—to name just a few professions that were closed or all but closed to women, just 50 years ago.

The world is better for the talent, worldview, and energy that women bring to those jobs. The church would be better with women priests for the same reason.

I am certain in my bones that, someday, maybe sooner rather than later, church leaders will come to a new understanding about what it means to be a priest. And will begin ordaining women.

A few days before she died, Janine was told that the archdiocese

‹‹ Janine risked and lost her religious home. ››

wouldn't permit her to be buried out of St. Gertrude. It was one more pain added onto the pain of her cancer and her imminent death. Janine risked and lost her religious home.

It was a kind of martyrdom. And, like the martyrs of old, her example is a shining light of hope for those of us she left behind.

PATRICK T. REARDON, baptized 1949, writer, St. Gertrude Parish in Edgewater.

The meaning of perfection

This story goes back to 1967, when the church was awash with the spirit of Vatican II. I had been a Sister of Mercy for twenty-one years and was teaching art at Mother McAuley Liberal Arts High School in Chicago. One evening I found in my cell a sheaf of mimeographed pages with a chapter of the constitution of St. Augustine printed at the top of each page. (The constitution lays out the principles of religious life for many orders, including ours.) We were asked to *comment* on the constitution. You *never* commented on the constitution. You obeyed it.

So I commented. The constitution's first sentence reads, "The object of the Institute is the perfection of its members according to the constitution." My comment: "It seems to me that, in practice, the object of the Institute is the perfection of the Institute."

Amazingly, a sister who had once been my superior before being promoted to the provincial council recognized my writing and called me in to explain. There were no ramifications, but I was flabbergasted at the breach of anonymity.

I have been out of religious life since 1970, married for 38 years to Tim Unsworth of *National Catholic Reporter* renown, and actively trying to make Vatican II the spirit of my life. Yet I continue to find that comment valid in light of the machinations of the papacy and the bishops. It explains the sexual abuse scandal, which revealed church fathers prioritizing the well-being of the institution above the men, women, and children who belonged to it. It explains the effort today to exert power in every way, even in small changes in the translation of the liturgy that force longtime churchgoers to consult the missal to say the Nicene Creed. It keeps us saying, "Yes" to the powers that be, saying, in effect, "We know you are still in charge."

If the church would recognize the original meaning in St. Augustine's rule, "the perfection of its members," Rome would be celebrating the sisters in America instead of investigating them to find any deviation from the papacy's idea of obedient sisters. Women religious today are serving the church in ways we never thought of when I was a Sister of Mercy. Theirs is an example to not only celebrate, but emulate.

JEAN MORMAN UNSWORTH, baptized 1925, Sister of Mercy, art teacher, author, wife, Loyola University professor of fine arts, St. Clement Church in Lincoln Park.

'Just like Hurricane Katrina'

"I'm not going back there," I said to my best friend through the phone, my tears rendering my speech nearly incomprehensible. I reached up to grab a wad of toilet paper from the roll and readjusted my feet, hoping that no one would find me sitting on the floor of the handicap stall. Had I really heard such a barbaric comment made in a class-room at a prominent graduate school of theology?

Walking into class that day, I had known I needed to brace myself for the discussion ahead. At the conclusion of the previous week's class, we had been assigned to read theologians Todd Salzman and Michael Lawler's progressive position on homosexuality and a number of counterarguments made by the magisterium. I sat down cautiously in my seat and waited for the professor to cue the questions that would guide our dialogue for three hours. The class seemed divided. Some of my classmates, mostly religious women, lay men and women, and religious men from Latin America had expressed discontent with the church's teachings on homosexuality; many of the white religious men, the majority in the class, defended Rome's infallible authority.

The professor, an expert in the area of Catholic sexual ethics, directed our attention to the contentious subject of the origin of homosexuality. In the field of ethics, the question of moral culpability, or sin, rests on the freedom to choose. Thus the discussion hinged on whether homosexuality was a choice or an intrinsic part of a person's sexual nature.

One student, Sr. Mary, pointed out that the catechism states that while the origin of homosexuality is unknown, the pastoral letter "Always Our Children" from the U.S. Conference of Catholic Bishops proclaims that homosexual orientation is not freely chosen. The latter statement, of course, removed culpability from the homosexual individual. The disconnect was obvious, and several classmates shot their hands into the air. They expressed their disappointment with a teaching that framed an orientation as blameless but condemned the acts that organically and lovingly flowed from it. Just as Anna, a lay woman, was voicing her frustration, another student, a religious brother and soon-to-be-ordained priest in the church, cut her off.

"Think of it this way," he said, his chest pushed out, refusing to look in Anna's direction. "It's just like Hurricane Katrina."

I'm from Florida. I saw Katrina firsthand. The wind toppled oaks across the roads in my neighborhood and ripped the roof off a house. I heard my friend shriek with desperation when she saw the first home she ever owned crushed by a tree. The horror of that storm is not, for me, an abstraction.

He continued.

"God created the hurricane, yes?" He paused and scanned the room for emphasis. "Well, no one would dare say *that* was a good thing."

Some of my classmates gasped. I felt the hatred in his words as my face turned red with disbelief and hurt. I turned to the professor hoping she would correct him. She did nothing. As the room sat in silence, I stood up and rushed to the door. I spent the rest of the class on the floor of that bathroom stall, trying and failing to grasp how even within the church, so many of us have failed to be true disciples of Christ.

MARIÁ SAPUCAHY BALATA, baptized 1985, theologian, ethicist, Archdiocesan Gay and Lesbian Outreach at Our Lady of Mount Carmel Church in Boystown.

Spelling 'archbishop'

Six Archbishops have headed the Chicago church in my life, four influenced by Vatican II. Soon will come a seventh. In my dreams, I see an ordinary whose character is as illustrious as his title.

A. Authenticity, genuineness, a person emulating "WYSIATI" (What-You-See-Is-All-There-Is). Attentive to archdiocesan culture.

R. Respect coupled with respectfulness. A "rabbi" or teacher who operates by listening, and more importantly, by hearing.

C. Creative, communicative, collaborative, creation-centered, a change-agent. Community, collegiality, and compassion are guiding principles.

H. As the archdiocese's heart, he promotes holiness, in the words of Vatican II's *Decree Concerning the Pastoral Office of Bishops in the Church*, by "counsel, persuasion, and example." The Holy Spirit is his guide.

B. Barriers of divisiveness are broken. Unity of being and becoming is lived. Belief—dynamic, organic, evolutionary—characterizes him.

I. Informed of the faithful's needs, including the needs of the separated and non-baptized. According to the same Vatican II decree, bishops should use the tools of social research "to become duly acquainted with their [the faithful's] needs in the social circumstances in which they live." Using contemporary social media, dialogue with society is initiated and promoted.

S. A scholar and a student of the 21st century. His spirituality is supported by scripture. A servant-leader, he is a superhero in the fight against sexism, especially ecclesiastical. He stands against all injustice.

H. Marked by holiness, he is a healer, a harmonizer. He honors freedom for informed consciences and exudes hope.

O. A preferential option for the poor and marginalized is evident, and openness marks his relationships.

P. Priests are trusted partners. Prophecy, pastoral practice, and living in the presence of God are hallmarks of his tenure. His priority: the good of the Lord's flock.

This looks like it spells "archbishop," but actually it's "saint"— what I crave.

JOAN KREBS, baptized 1930, mostly retired, small discussion group facilitator, registered tax preparer, associate in the Congregation of St. Joseph in La Grange Park, family member, friend of many, St. Mary of the Woods Catholic Church in Edgebrook.

A rude awakening

I am a member of St. Cornelius parish in Jefferson Park in Chicago. I have been a member of St. Cornelius since birth and had the sacraments of baptism, reconciliation, and First Communion at St. Cornelius. I am an altar server, I sing in the choir, and I go to religious education.

When I was eight, our pastor retired. Then we got an acting pastor who had to leave. Then another acting pastor announced in church one Sunday that our new pastor was Father Dan. Sitting in church I realized all of the pastors that we had had were men. I crinkled my eyebrows together and asked my mother, "Why is it never a woman?" She looked upset and said, "We'll talk later, but I have to tell you something, and you're not going to like it."

On the way home my mother told me that a woman could not become a Catholic priest. I was really upset. I had heard stories about medieval days where girls were treated like possessions, told they had nothing in their heads, and they weren't allowed to learn. I read a story about girls in the Revolutionary War who had to take care of other children and the house and couldn't do what the boys could do, like fight. I read a story about a girl whose mother was a suffragette and how her mom was trying to get equal rights and the vote.

In 2008, when I was eight, there wasn't much of that still going on. Sure, there was still the percentage that men got paid more than women, but it wasn't like a woman couldn't be a teacher or a doctor or a physicist or rule a country. When I heard that the Catholic church wouldn't have women as priests I couldn't even think of another example where women weren't equal to men. It was a rude awakening because it made me realize there were still people who didn't allow women to do things just because they were born a girl instead of a boy.

Later my mom told me stories about when she was a little girl. She couldn't be an altar server, but my uncle was head of the altar boys. That made me feel that women in the church had progressed a bit.

I am going to be twelve soon. I'm still really upset that women can't do more in the church. Last year during religious education class I found out the reason a woman can't be a priest or a bishop is because an earlier pope made an edict. Jesus didn't say it. Even though a lot of people might not acknowledge it, I think Jesus was trying to bring women into his close circle, like he brought Mary Magdalene.

If girls couldn't be altar servers, but now they can, we can still make progress. There are priests who think women could be priests and bishops and cardinals. I think change is going to come someday. I hope that day comes sooner rather than later.

MAIRI GLYNN, baptized 2000, sixth-grade student at Skinner West Elementary School, St. Cornelius Catholic Church in Jefferson Park.

Salvaging the remnants

The last year I worked as a pastoral associate in Arlington Heights I noticed that in the alleyway between the church and rectory, a group of industrious robins had made a nest. In the church gutter lay a home of twigs and broken branches interspersed with pieces of shiny ribbon, nylon netting, tulle, and other remnants collected from the church steps after weddings. I thought: How clever are God's winged creatures to make such a lovely home from the scraps of the church where they live.

I am a woman, called to minister to God's people in my faith tradition. From a very young age my love of Eucharist formed my being. As the mother of five children, I fed to my young God's word and promise. How fortunate I felt to be raising my family and serving my church in the years following Vatican II. The windows of inclusivity, God's mercy, and compassion were wide open. Here was a place to build a home for the next generation. I studied scripture, liturgy, sacraments, liberation theology, prayer, preaching—life was full. My nest was expansive.

As the children grew, so did I. Called to pray with the dying, sing with the children, catechize, welcome, build. I was blessed, graced with opportunities, privileged to use my gifts to serve my church.

Then slowly, things changed. The sex abuse scandal. The death of Cardinal Bernardin. The leadership tasks of parish life that I and female associates from other churches previously had undertaken

‹‹ **The windows of compassion were wide open.** ››

were handed off to ordained men. Windows closed. Language was revised. Edicts were issued. Paranoia surfaced. Orthodoxy developed. Respect evaporated. Rank ruled. Feminism shriveled. Fear took over the home.

Today I pray for my six beautiful granddaughters and the loss of their rightful inheritance. I think of the robins, and how I am like them, how for the last ten years I have tried to recreate a home in my church from the fragments of treasures I collected during the first 50 years. I wish I possessed a fraction of the birds' ingenuity.

MARLENE SWEENEY, baptized 1948, writer, former pastoral associate, member of St. Hubert Parish in Hoffman Estates.

REDEMPTION

A bishop who made a difference

Published in Chicago's paper of record, 2031.

Holy Name Cathedral had standing room only Tuesday for the funeral of Archbishop Jude Goodman. Loudspeakers outside accommodated the throngs on the street who could not get in. During his 12 years as Chicago's Catholic leader, Goodman had a profound effect on the city and its Catholic population.

Perhaps his most significant contribution was his requirement that all candidates for the position of pastor be interviewed by leaders of the receiving congregation and be voted in by the entire parish before taking the position. The archbishop insisted he was only following the rule that once guided the church for almost a millennium: "The one who leads all shall be chosen by all."

Working in collaboration with his priests, Goodman introduced the practice of decision-making parish councils in place of the customary advisory council. Many said it couldn't be done, but Archbishop Goodman, who personally worked for years with laity and pastors in every vicariate, insisted broad lay participation was necessary. Today, such bodies exist in virtually every Chicago parish, though problems are still being ironed out.

Then of course it was Goodman who convinced church leaders that the time had come to ordain women as deacons. Since their introduction two years ago, thousands of parishes in the United States and around the world are welcoming women into diaconal roles, including preaching, baptizing, and anointing. He is also the one who persuaded church leaders to launch discussions on women priests, contraception, and gay rights. Discussions are ongoing.

The archbishop crossed borders as none of his predecessors had by working on common social concerns with Protestants, Jews, Muslims, and other believers, by sponsoring ecumenical and interfaith services, and by encouraging the sharing of pulpits on a regular basis. He also met with GLBT groups and with leaders of the Women's Ordination Conference. He even attended the ordination of a woman last year, explaining afterward, "I had to go. She is a dear friend."

Goodman came to be known as "Jude the Listener," due to his unique ability to take everyone seriously, engage in stimulating conversation, and hear their position without interruption or contradiction. "We don't always agree," he said, "but we part as friends."

Archbishop Goodman was called to Rome four times to explain his innovations but always returned victorious with a new concession from the Holy Father. He was offered the red hat but declined, saying he thought the idea of a college of "princes parading around in medieval costumes was both ludicrous and completely out of sync with the style of our founder." His last request, that priests and bishops attending his funeral dress simply and not make the event "a liturgical circus," was honored by all present.

ROBERT MCCLORY, baptized 1932, writer, retired university professor, husband, father of one, St. Nicholas Church in Evanston.

Another Chicago fire

I believe that God wants Chicago to be united in the love of God. I hope and pray that the Catholic church will play a major role in a widespread unifying return to holiness in our urban area.

About 15 years ago, I was blessed with my life's only vision: a map of Chicago with many small flames about it, then bursting into a single larger flame. Three weeks prior to receiving that vision, I had been on pilgrimage with my wife, a trip that included the Cave of the Revelation on the Greek island of Patmos where St. John received his inspiration. I put my hand on that sacred ceiling and prayed that I would know and do the Lord's will in my life. Three weeks later back in Chicago, I was in prayer thinking about that experience when I received the vision. Then about ten years later, while once again in prayer, I understood the title of the vision to be: "Our City Aflame with the Love of God."

The Holy Spirit is mightily at work touching hearts and lives so that "igniters" will encourage strong believers—whether Catholic, Protestant, Jewish, Muslim, or perhaps other faith traditions as well—to share their love of God. What seems irreconcilable to us, who are normally divided by limits of mere religion, will be shattered. Christians of all persuasions will feel the unity, though it may take a while to "trickle up" to our religious hierarchy in the Catholic church. Meanwhile, various other believers will emerge in harmony to fulfill common needs and work for the common good.

‹‹ God wants Chicago to be united in the love of God. ››

This focus will be attractive to many, and even the current strong pull of secular society will seem trivial in comparison. God is bringing us together in unprecedented ways to serve the common good for his honor and glory.

ALLEN STRYCZEK, baptized 1951, retired certified project manager, St. Gertrude Parish in Edgewater.

Truly present

Our Lord loves to teach us about the wonders and mysteries of his church. I've seen it personally.

When I was in my thirties, I was browsing in a Catholic bookstore and felt moved to purchase a book on Eucharistic miracles. I read how in 700 A.D. in Lanciano, Italy, a Basilian monk was struggling to maintain his belief in transubstantiation. The monk cried out to the Lord to strengthen his rapidly waning faith. Much like the Apostle Thomas, he needed to see, feel, and experience the Truth in a more physical way.

When he said the words of Consecration at his next Mass, the host transformed into human flesh, and the wine turned into human blood right there on the altar. The pope proclaimed it a miracle, and the Body and Blood of our Lord was painstakingly safeguarded through the centuries.

In the 1970s, Pope John Paul II hired top European scientists to analyze the miracle. What they discovered transcended science. The host was made of human heart tissue from the myocardium, and the scientists said it was impossible for a person to cut out such a perfect disc from a heart. When they tested the five clumps of blood, they saw something even more amazing. Though human blood begins to decompose within minutes, when they added water, it became fresh again. The lead scientist, an agnostic at the time, sent a personal telegram to the Holy Father, saying, "In the beginning was the Word, and the Word was made flesh."

When I read this I prayed to the Lord asking to see this miracle someday and maybe get a chance to visit St. Peter's as well. At the time I was director of operations for a large manufacturer. Within days, my European counterpart, Franco, called to ask if I could travel overseas to speak about some of our successes in the States.

All our company's meetings were held at headquarters in England, so I asked if he wanted me to fly into Heathrow Airport.

"No, we want to do something different this year," he said. "We are going to fly into Rome."

I then asked if he had ever heard of a town called Lanciano. It was a small town off the Adriatic, he said, and right by where the meeting would be held.

But then my schedule unexpectedly changed. I was told the jammed schedule of the chief executive officer whom I was supposed to meet made it impossible to reschedule. The visit was off. Yet I hung up the phone with a smile, thinking, "I can't wait to see how the Lord will work this out." A couple of days later, Franco called back to say that, amazingly, the CEO's schedule had changed. It now perfectly coincided with mine.

A few weeks later Franco and I were driving on cobblestone streets following signs that read *Miracolo Eucaristico* until we arrived at a non-descript church. The pastor led us to a glass case holding the monstrance and chalice which contained the precious Body and Blood of our risen Lord.

I waited until I was alone at the altar. I dropped to my knees and asked the Lord to teach me something since he had led me such a long way to witness this miracle. As I beheld his countenance but inches from my face, I heard him speak.

"I have performed this miracle so that the world would know that whenever any one of my priests says the words of Consecration, the bread and wine truly become my Flesh and my Blood," he said. "However, I must leave it in the form of bread and wine, for if I did not leave it in the form of bread and wine, you would not be able to consume me, and you would not be able to have my life within you."

The Lord had brought me a long way so that I could understand, not just intellectually, but on a gut level, that he was truly present in the Eucharist. I had been like a blind man listening to a description of a sunset; now I could see. I pray our next archbishop will see as well, will work to promulgate this deeply felt understanding of Christ's presence in the Eucharist, for if people truly understood what they received at Mass, the churches would overflow.

LEO MIKLIUS, baptized in 1955, husband and father of seven children, general manager, catechist for twenty-two years, St. Theresa Parish in Palatine.

Church and city

The Kingdom needs a church
That is, a city needs a place to gather,
A people needs a parish
It takes two wings to fly.

And speaking of birds, I have a calico cat.
Brindled and curious she sits on the window sill
Pondering the great outdoors, the promised land;
Hoping for and fearing that the window of opportunity

Where the red accept the blue, and the straight hail the bent,
Those who don't give a dream listen
To those who are heaven sent.
Our city is divided for those who have no hope,

Our parishes are divided for those who are kept out,
The church is now divided, brindled at the pane
Hoping and fearing what would be if we leapt out
It takes two wings to fly.

It's always a risk to explain a poem. And yet. I would like to see a brindled archbishop for my city, a multi-colored cardinal, a calico church leader. One who has read Studs Terkel's *Division Street*; who believes in unions, loving and at the table; who can straddle and bridge; who

‹‹ I would like to see a calico church leader. ››

considers Chicago home, not Rome; who goes to our plays, movies, and symphonies; likes hot dogs and pizza; and dislikes tired pieties. But especially we need an archbishop who is willing to make a leap of faith out the window, spending two or three days at each parish, living at the rectory, meeting the staff, gathering the people.

And, yes, he should walk the parish dog. It's good for the heart.

FATHER BILL KENNEALLY, baptized 1935, retired pastor of St. Gertrude, St. Barnabas Parish in Beverly.

The spirit of the law

I got the news while on a business trip: Jon, the 37-year-old son of my office manager, Donna, had died by suicide in the family home in Chicago. I called her a few minutes later. Was there anything I could do?

Yes, she said. She'd like to have Jon's funeral at a Catholic church on the North Side. Could I help arrange it? Yes, of course I could (although I had no idea how).

I was surprised at the request, since Donna had been severely hurt by a Catholic priest many years ago who told her she was going to hell because she had her tubes tied after having her second child. And Jon was not exactly what you would call your typical Catholic. He was gay and suffered from severe bipolar disease and had an incredibly irreverent sense of humor. Neither had been a practicing Catholic for many years, despite having attended Catholic schools and having two nuns in the family.

Jon had worked briefly for my company, until he had one of his manic episodes and became convinced that he had received over the Internet a job offer to be the singer Madonna's personal photographer. He quit and moved to Los Angeles, where he lost everything and became homeless and was eventually incarcerated. His mother and father worked ceaselessly to get him home, and finally—with the help of Illinois' then Lt. Governor Pat Quinn—succeeded. Jon tried hard to overcome his mental illness for the sake of his family, but he eventually succumbed to the pain of just being alive, leaving a note asking them to forgive him.

Forgive him they did, and now they were asking the church to do the same. I have a lot of priest friends in the Archdiocese of Chicago, and when I called the first one on the list, Father Bill Kenneally, the recently retired pastor of St. Gertrude's parish on the North Side, and explained the situation, he did not hesitate. "Of course, I'll say the

Mass," he said, "and I'll take care of getting the church." All he asked was that he be given the opportunity to visit with the family before the funeral and that I give the eulogy for Jon.

The wake was on the night of one of the worst snowstorms of the year, but the priest drove all the way from the Beverly neighborhood on the far South Side, met the family, said a prayer over Jon, and drove back home through the storm. The next day was the funeral, and everyone showed up at St. Gertrude's, a church most of them had never entered before. The liturgy and music were beautiful, Father Kenneally presided with warmth and sensitivity, I gave the eulogy, and Donna went to communion for the first time in decades.

I thought afterwards that there had been a redemption here, but it wasn't only of Donna and Jon and their family. It was redemption of the church itself—the church that had browbeat a young woman for doing what she thought was best for her family, the church that had communicated to her son that there was something wrong with his sexual orientation. It was this same church that stepped up and did what Jesus always asked us to do: Love one another as he loved us. That is the Chicago church at its best, following the spirit rather than the letter of the law.

GREGORY F. AUGUSTINE PIERCE, baptized 1947, book publisher and former president of the National Center for the Laity, St. Mary of the Woods Catholic Church in Edgebrook, where his wife, Kathy, teaches seventh and eighth grade.

Urbs in horto

"Céad mile fáilte!" As archbishop you enjoy a privileged position of seeing our church at its best. Whenever you visit our parishes, you see shining communities. Your presence draws out the good in all of us: Choirs sing as well as they are able, maintenance crews polish our facilities, and societies offer amazing hospitality and welcome.

I encourage you to build upon this ability to bring out the best. Our archdiocese has great strengths: Vibrant parishes proclaiming the Gospel with joy, a school system educating thousands, a medical care system blanketing the area, and an awesome outreach of charity to those in dire need.

But our Archdiocese also has not squarely faced many issues: Demographic shifts leaving shells of parishes, schools with unhealthy enrollments, financial decisions put off for a future day. With your arrival, that day has dawned. A process of healthy pruning must begin. Remember that only the best will do. Engage us in new ways of thinking that respond to current realities. Bring imagination and decisiveness into our visioning and planning. Set goals and new directions. Join your voice to those of others of goodwill who call out for a better Chicago: one that is less violent and politically corrupt, more tolerant and open. As you draw out the best in each one of us, enabling our dreams, vocalizing an energized vision, preaching the Gospel with humility and love, what a blossoming our local church will experience. As archbishop you will help us live up to our civic motto: *Urbs in horto*, a city in a garden.

Enjoy your years with us. Stroll along the lakefront and through the Chicago Botanic Garden; sit on the lawn at the Pritzker Pavilion or at Ravinia for an al fresco concert; absorb masterpieces at the Art Institute and local theaters; delight in music from a world-class symphony and the Lyric Opera; appreciate the verve of ethnic life, like a "football" match on the pitch of Gaelic Park. Cheer on our local sports teams in good times and bad. Immerse yourself in the life of this great area. We love our city, and in time you will see why we do. Above all, in all of this, get to know our wonderful people. You will come to love them, as they love the Lord. You remain in our prayers. "A hundred thousand welcomes!" Now, get to work.

REV. WILLIAM T. CORCORAN, PH.D., baptized 1956, pastor, St. Linus Parish in Oak Lawn.